Managing The Micromanager

Basant Prasad

SPI Publications

Published by **SPI Publications**, www.spipublications.in

SPI, the **SPI logo**, and **Split Poetry India** are trademarks of **SPI Publications**, or its affiliates.

ISBN-13: 978-93-49860-05-6

First Edition 2025

SPI Publications

Corporate & Editorial Office

117/2, Sector 37, Khandsa Road,
Gurgaon, Haryana 122 001
Phone: +91 98355 52940
Email: contact@spipublications.in
Website: www.spipublications.in

Processed and Printed in India

Preface

A Survival Guide for the Over-Supervised

Let's be honest. If you picked up this book, you probably have one. Or perhaps you've had several throughout your career. That person who, despite your best efforts, seems to have an invisible umbilical cord attached directly to your workflow.

The one who asks for updates on tasks you just started five minutes ago. The one who offers "helpful" suggestions that are actually just thinly veiled instructions on how to do your job, even though you've been doing it for years. Yes, we're talking about the micromanager.

You know them. You might even be one, secretly (and if so, welcome! We've got insights for you too). But for most of us, being on the receiving end of micromanagement feels like trying to run a marathon with someone constantly tying your shoelaces.

It's frustrating. It's demoralizing. It stifles creativity, crushes autonomy, and can make even the most passionate professional dream of a career as a hermit.

I've been there. I've lived through the endless check-ins, the nitpicking over minor details, the feeling of being constantly doubted and undermined. And through those experiences, and by observing countless others, I've come to a crucial realization: micromanagement isn't just a personality quirk.

It's a dynamic, a dance between two (or more) people, and like any dance, you can learn new steps. You can change the rhythm. You can even lead.

This book is not about complaining. (Though, let's be real, a good vent session is always welcome.) This book is a practical, no-nonsense, and hopefully, occasionally humorous guide to navigating the challenging landscape of micromanagement.

It's a survival guide, a strategy manual, and a toolkit for reclaiming your autonomy, boosting your productivity, and restoring your sanity.

We're going to dissect the micromanager – not to demonize them, but to understand them. Because understanding is the first step towards effective management (yes, you'll be managing them).

We'll explore the psychological drivers behind their behavior, the impact it has on you and your team, and most importantly, the actionable strategies you can employ to shift the dynamic.

This isn't about confrontation or rebellion (unless strategically necessary, of course). It's about subtle shifts, clear communication, proactive measures, and building trust. It's about becoming so reliably excellent, so proactively communicative, and so clearly in control of your domain that the micromanager feels less need to hover. It's about creating an environment where their anxiety is soothed, and your freedom is expanded.

So, if you're tired of feeling suffocated, undervalued, and perpetually under the microscope, grab a beverage, settle in, and let's turn that frustrating dynamic into an opportunity for growth – for both you and your micromanager. Your autonomy awaits.

Contents

Chapter 1: Understanding the Beast – What Makes a Micromanager Tick? 7

Chapter 2: The Art of Pre-Emptive Strikes — Communicating Before You're Asked 14

Chapter 3: Setting Boundaries Without Burning Bridges 22

Chapter 4: Building Trust – One Small Win at a Time 28

Chapter 5: Surviving the Long Game – Resilience in the Micromanagement Zone 34

Chapter 6: Stealth Mode – Influencing Without Triggering Alarms. 40

Chapter 7: Breaking the Cycle – Becoming the Manager You Always Wanted 45

Chapter 9: Digital Chains – Micromanagement in the Remote Era 56

Chapter 10: When to Fold 'Em – Recognizing When It's Time to Leave 63

Chapter 11: Life After the Microscope – Thriving Beyond Micromanagement 68

Chapter 1: Understanding the Beast – What Makes a Micromanager Tick?

Alright, let's kick things off by getting into the head of the beast. Before we can effectively manage a micromanager, we need to understand what makes them tick. It's like trying to fix a leaky faucet without knowing where the water supply is. You can frantically mop up the floor all day, but the problem will persist.

Micromanagement isn't typically born out of malice. It's rarely a grand scheme to make your life miserable (though it certainly feels that way sometimes, doesn't it?). More often, it stems from a complex mix of anxieties, past experiences, and sometimes, even a misguided attempt to be helpful.

So, let's put on our amateur psychologist hats and explore the common culprits behind this particular brand of supervisory behavior.

The Root Causes: Why Do They Do It?

Understanding the "why" behind the micromanagement is crucial. It allows you to approach the situation with a degree of empathy (yes, I know, it's hard sometimes!) and, more importantly, to tailor your strategies to address the underlying cause, rather than just reacting to the symptoms.

1. Anxiety and Fear (The Worried Watchdog)

This is, arguably, the biggest driver of micromanagement. Your micromanager is probably scared. Scared of what?.

Fear of Failure: They might be terrified of their own failure, and they see your work as a direct reflection of their success. If your project goes sideways, they might believe it makes them look bad to their superiors. This isn't about your competence; it's about their insecurity.

Fear of Losing Control: In a world that often feels chaotic and unpredictable, micromanaging provides a sense of control. By overseeing every detail, they feel like they're minimizing risks and ensuring everything goes according to their plan.

Fear of the Unknown: They might lack trust in the process, the team, or even their own ability to delegate effectively. The unknown is scary, and controlling the known (even the tiny knowns) offers a false sense of security.

Pressure from Above: Sometimes, the micromanager themselves is being micromanaged. Pressure trickles down. If their boss is breathing down their neck for every detail, they might, consciously or unconsciously, pass that pressure onto you. They're just a cog in a larger, anxious machine.

2. Lack of Trust (The Skeptical Supervisor)

This can be a tough pill to swallow, but sometimes micromanagement stems from a genuine (though often unfounded) lack of trust in your abilities, your judgment, or your commitment.

Past Negative Experiences: They might have been let down by a previous employee, a past team, or even themselves. This negative experience has hardwired them to be overly cautious and to assume that if they don't oversee everything, things will inevitably go wrong.

Inexperience with Delegation: Some managers have never been taught how to delegate effectively. They might believe that "managing" means "doing it yourself, but through others," rather than empowering their team. They don't trust the outcome unless they've touched every piece of it.

Perceived Competence Gap: They might genuinely believe they are the only one capable of doing the task "correctly." This isn't necessarily a slight against you; it might be an inflated sense of their own indispensability or a lack of understanding of your capabilities.

3. Perfectionism (The Detail Devil)

For some micromanagers, it's all about the details. They have an exceptionally high standard (sometimes unrealistically high) and believe that the only way to meet it is to scrutinize every single step.

Aversion to Errors: They might have a very low tolerance for mistakes, seeing even minor errors as catastrophic failures. This drives them to meticulously check and re-check everything.

Process Obsession: They might be more focused on how something is done rather than what is achieved. Their comfort comes from adherence to a specific process, even if there are more efficient ways to get to the same result.

"My Way or the Highway" Mentality: They might genuinely believe their way is the only right way to do something, even if your approach is equally effective or even better. This can stifle innovation and creativity.

4. Lack of Self-Awareness (The Unknowing Nudger)

Perhaps the most frustrating type of micromanager is the one who has no idea they're doing it. They genuinely believe they are being helpful, supportive, or simply "engaged."

"Just Checking In": They might see their constant check-ins as proactive communication or a sign of their availability, not as intrusive hovering.

"Leading by Example": They might believe they are modeling diligence and attention to detail, unaware that it's stifling their team's autonomy.

Positive Intent, Negative Impact: Their intentions might be good (e.g., "I want to make sure they succeed," "I want to catch problems early"), but they're blind to the negative impact of their behavior on team morale, productivity, and retention.

5. Over-Reliance on Old Habits (The Stuck-in-the-Mud Manager)

They might have been promoted from a role where being detail-oriented and hands-on was a strength. Now, in a managerial role, they haven't adjusted their habits.

Individual Contributor Mindset: They still think like an individual contributor, believing their value comes from doing tasks rather than enabling others to do them.

Comfort in the Familiar: It's easier to revert to old habits, even if they're no longer effective, than to learn new managerial skills like delegation and empowerment.

The Impact on You: Why It's So Draining

Understanding their motivations doesn't make the experience any less frustrating. Micromanagement has tangible, negative impacts on you and your work:

Reduced Autonomy: You feel like a robot, just executing commands, rather than a thinking, contributing professional. This crushes job satisfaction.

Stifled Creativity and Innovation: When every step is dictated, there's no room to experiment, to find better ways, or to bring your unique perspective to a problem.

Lowered Morale and Motivation: Constant oversight signals a lack of trust, which is incredibly demotivating. Why put in extra effort if it's just going to be nitpicked?

Increased Stress and Anxiety: The constant feeling of being watched, judged, or doubted creates a high-pressure environment that leads to stress, anxiety, and even burnout.

Decreased Productivity (Yes, Really!): While micromanagers aim for control, they often achieve the opposite. Their constant interruptions, redundant checks, and demands for unnecessary updates actually slow down work and waste everyone's time.

Skill Stagnation: If you're never given the space to make decisions or learn from mistakes, your skills won't develop. You become reliant on the micromanager, creating a self-fulfilling prophecy.

Resentment: Over time, the frustration can fester into deep resentment, making the working relationship almost unbearable.

Your First Step: Observation, Not Judgment

Now that we've explored the "why" behind micromanagement, your first step isn't to confront, or to complain, or to plot your escape (though that might come later!). Your first step is to become an astute observer.

Identify the Triggers: When does the micromanagement intensify? Is it during high-stakes projects? When deadlines are looming? When they're feeling stressed? When you're working on something new?

Identify Their Specific Behaviors: Are they asking for hourly updates? Rewriting your emails? Demanding unnecessary reports? Hovering over your shoulder? Focusing on process over outcome?

Look for Patterns: Do these behaviors change depending on the project, the time of day, or their mood?.

Consider Their Past: Have they recently had a bad experience? Are they new to management?

This observation phase is crucial. It moves you from feeling like a victim to becoming a strategist. It allows you to understand their "language" and identify the specific anxieties or habits you'll need to address. Remember, you're not judging them; you're gathering intelligence.

In the next chapter, we'll move from understanding the beast to subtly taming it. We'll dive into the power of proactive communication – how to give your micromanager exactly what they need (and sometimes, what they don't even know they need) before they even have a chance to ask for it. Get ready to become a master of pre-emptive strikes!.

Chapter 2: The Art of Pre-Emptive Strikes — Communicating Before You're Asked

So, you've done your homework. You've spent some time watching the micromanager in their natural habitat. You know when their anxiety spikes. You've mapped out their habits, their triggers, and maybe even their secret hand signals (well, maybe not the last one, but you get the idea).

Now, what's next?

Now, it's time to turn from victim to tactician — to become that rare breed of professional who doesn't just wait for the next "How's this going?" email or the inevitable "Can I see a report?" demand.

Instead, you step boldly into the role of anticipation artist, delivering exactly what your micromanager needs — before they even realize they need it.

This, dear reader, is the art of the pre-emptive strike. But don't let the military metaphor fool you; this isn't about warfare. It's about deft diplomacy, building trust, and reclaiming your autonomy with finesse.

Mastering this approach requires patience, observation, and a bit of psychology, but the payoff is immense. It's about shifting the power dynamic without confrontation. It's about reducing your manager's anxiety by giving them the reassurance they crave — on your terms.

1. Know Their Information Diet – Feed Them What They Really Want

Every micromanager has an appetite for information — but the kind, quantity, and format vary wildly.

Some may crave daily updates sent via email. Others might prefer quick, informal chats during breaks or a brief phone call. Still others want detailed spreadsheets, charts, or even a shared dashboard that lays out progress in real-time.

Your first order of business is figuring out exactly what their "menu" looks like. Are they more of a "bullet points and brevity" type, or do they want deep dives packed with stats and minutiae? Do they want to receive updates via instant message, email, phone call, or in person?

Pro tip: If the format isn't clear, ask subtly. A simple, "Would you prefer a quick summary email or a short call at the end of the day?" signals your willingness to accommodate without revealing you're trying to decode their micromanagement style.

Why this matters: Drowning them in irrelevant details overwhelms and frustrates them — not to mention wastes your time. But starving them of information feeds their anxiety, creating a vacuum quickly filled with incessant requests and check-ins.

Feeding them just the right amount — delivered in the format that feels comfortable and familiar — reduces their urge to hover and gives you breathing room to focus on your work.

2. Build Your Reporting Rhythm – Become Predictable, Not Profitable (to Stress)

Micromanagers thrive on predictability, because it reduces their anxiety. When they know exactly when and how updates will arrive, their stress tends to ease.

This is your opportunity to create a reporting cadence — a steady, reliable drumbeat that calms the waters.

Once you've identified how often your micromanager wants updates, stick to that schedule religiously. If they want a twice-weekly update, send it on the same days each week, at roughly the same time. If daily check-ins are their jam, frame it as a brief, consistent ritual rather than a chaotic scramble.

Bonus move: Include a forward-looking element in every update. Instead of just recounting what happened, preview what's coming next:

"This week, I plan to complete X by Wednesday, and Y is scheduled for Friday."

This signals not only control but foresight — two things micromanagers desperately crave but often find lacking.

3. Anticipate Their Concerns – Become Their Friendly Neighborhood Problem-Solver

If a micromanager were a movie director, your work would be "dailies" — fragments of a larger story they're scrutinizing for potential disaster scenes. They're constantly scanning for what could go wrong. When they spot a problem early, they can revert their anxiety levels closer to "functional."

You can become their MVP by identifying potential issues before they do and flagging them with a proposed solution.

Example:

- "I noticed the supplier might delay shipment by two days due to weather, but I'm working on a secondary vendor to mitigate this."
- "Our resource allocation for Task A appears tight, so I'm coordinating with Team B to shuffle priorities if needed."

This tactic transforms you from the object of constant surveillance into a trusted troubleshooter. Rather than triggering alarm bells with surprises, you become the person who brings problem-solving to the table preemptively.

Important caveat: Never just drop a problem in their lap without context or a plan. Micromanagers love to fix things — give them the chance, but make sure it's on your terms, so you retain agency.

4. Speak Their Language – Communicate in the Vernacular of Their Concerns

Communication isn't just about what you say; it's about how and in what terms you say it.

Each micromanager has their own vocabulary of concerns and metrics. If your manager is obsessed with ROI, productivity, or risk reduction, frame your updates around those metrics.

Instead of:

"I completed the client proposal, and I think it looks good."

Try:

"The client proposal is completed ahead of schedule, with projected ROI exceeding our target by 8%, minimizing risk due to our new vendor terms."

By mirroring their language and placing your progress within their conceptual framework, you lower mental defenses. Your updates become relevant and reassuring instead of just noise.

This doesn't mean losing your voice or authenticity — it's about wrapping your work narrative in terms that resonate with their anxieties and goals.

5. Create an Information Dashboard – Transparency Without Interruption

If your work involves measurable progress — think project completions, sales pipelines, bug fixes — consider creating a simple dashboard or shared document.

This acts like a self-service portal for your manager, letting them check status updates anytime without needing to interrupt your workflow.

Ground rules:

- Keep it clean and easy to read — no clutter.
- Update it regularly before your scheduled reports.
- Focus on key data points they care about.

This transparency gives them the illusion of control at their fingertips, which often slashes their need to hover or demand constant status checks.

6. Over-Communicate (But Not Too Much) – Finding the Sweet Spot

Over-communication here means proactive, relevant, and timely updates — not a nonstop flood of minute-by-minute reports.

It's the difference between an executive summary that gives them what they need and a transcription of every keystroke you make.

Striking this balance will likely require some trial and error, and the easiest way to find the sweet spot is to ask:

"Would you prefer a quick weekly update or daily detailed reports?"

This question respects their preference and signals you're taking control of the flow, not leaving it to chance.

7. Check In Without Being Asked – Sending Tiny Confidence Flags

Proactive check-ins can be a game-changer. When you accomplish a significant milestone or detect a minor obstacle, send a brief message or call just to signal you're on top of it.

Think of this as a tiny flag waving a reassuring "All clear here!" or "Heads up — I'm handling a small hiccup."

This small gesture builds confidence over time, reducing the urge for your micromanager to intrude.

8. Manage Your Own Emotional Radar – Confidence Is Contagious

Managing a micromanager isn't just about managing them — it's also about managing you.

When you take control of communication — when you proactively report, anticipate concerns, and speak their language — you also gain greater control over your own emotions.

Instead of stewing over every interruption, you'll gain a sense of forward momentum and agency. Calm, steady confidence often rubs off, coaxing them to dial back their need to hover.

Putting It All Together — Your Pre-Emptive Playbook

- **Scout their information diet** — Know typc, format, and frequency.
- **Establish a reliable reporting rhythm** — Predictability reduces anxiety.
- **Flag potential issues early — with solutions** — Become a trusted problem solver.
- **Speak in their language** — Use their metrics and terms.
- **Create transparency** — Dashboards or shared docs for self-service updates.
- **Balance communication frequency** — Avoid overload and scarcity.
- **Initiate check-ins proactively** — Small "confidence flags."
- **Manage your emotional landscape** — Calmness inspires calmness.

Reality check: This won't cure micromanagement overnight — habits and anxieties run deep. But it shifts you from reactive mode into leading the dance. And that makes all the difference.

Chapter 3: Setting Boundaries Without Burning Bridges

Boundaries. The word itself sounds like something from a therapy session or a corporate HR workshop. But when you're dealing with a micromanager, boundaries aren't just a nice-to-have — they're a survival tool. Think of them as emotional fences that protect your sanity, productivity, and confidence.

But here's the tricky part: setting boundaries with a micromanager is not the same as dealing with a regular colleague or friend. These are people who thrive on control, who equate constant involvement with effectiveness, and who often have no idea they're even crossing lines. So, if you're going to set boundaries, you'll need a blend of tact, clarity, consistency, and (let's be honest) some Jedi-level diplomacy.

Let's walk through how to assert yourself without triggering World War III in your office.

Identify Your Line in the Sand: What's Non-Negotiable?

Before you can communicate boundaries, you need to know where they are. Not all micromanagement behaviors will drive you equally nuts. What is it that truly affects your ability to work — or your wellbeing?

Maybe it's the 10 PM texts. Maybe it's being cc'd on every email. Maybe it's surprise video calls asking for status updates when you're deep in flow.

Make a mental (or literal) list. Knowing your pressure points helps you be specific later on — and avoids vague feedback that gets ignored.

Use Assertive, Not Aggressive, Communication

Micromanagers are often hyper-sensitive to perceived defiance. So, when communicating boundaries, tone is everything. You're not laying down the law; you're inviting collaboration for more effective work.

Instead of:

"Please stop messaging me late at night. It's really disruptive."

Try:

"I've found I do my best thinking and most efficient work during the day. To stay fresh and focused, I try to disconnect from work messages after 7 PM. Can we align on handling non-urgent items the next morning?"

You're asserting a need while also offering a reasonable framework. This feels less like a wall and more like a guided walkway.

Offer Alternatives Instead of Just Shutting Doors

Micromanagers often react poorly to boundaries because they interpret them as a lack of control. The trick? Give them something else to feel in control of.

If they ask for updates constantly, propose a structured format:

"Instead of multiple check-ins throughout the day, I can send a summary email at 4 PM with everything completed and what's planned for tomorrow. That way, you're in the loop and I can stay focused."

This replaces chaos with clarity. You're not saying "no" — you're offering a better way.

Be Consistent: Repetition Builds Respect

The first time you set a boundary, your micromanager may test it. The second time, they might forget. By the third time, it becomes part of your working relationship — if you're consistent.

If you said you don't take work calls after hours, don't pick up. If you agreed on weekly updates, don't jump to send daily ones when they ask "just this once."

Consistency tells them: "This isn't a phase. This is how I work best." It sets a standard they begin to adapt to — even if begrudgingly.

Frame Boundaries Around Productivity and Value

Micromanagers care deeply about results. So frame your boundaries as enablers of better performance — not personal preferences.

"When I have a few uninterrupted hours in the morning, I'm able to get twice as much strategic work done. Can we block that time as heads-down focus time?"

Or:

"Reviewing work in batches helps me provide better quality and catch more details. Can we reserve feedback for the end of the day instead of real-time comments?"

You're showing them the boundary is a productivity strategy, not a rebellion.

Enlist Allies (Quietly and Strategically)

Sometimes the best way to reinforce boundaries is through subtle support. If you have a mentor, HR rep, or trusted colleague who understands your situation, let them know what you're trying to do. They can back you up in meetings or help reinforce new norms.

Just be careful not to turn it into gossip — this isn't about staging a coup. It's about making sure your reasonable requests echo louder than the micromanagement noise.

Know When to Escalate (and When Not To)

If your micromanager crosses into disrespectful or toxic behavior — public shaming, gaslighting, or nonstop 24/7 demands — then boundary-setting alone may not be enough. In these cases, document what's happening and consider involving HR or a trusted senior leader.

But if the issue is more garden-variety hovering and over-involvement, keep your escalation tools in your back pocket for now. Try the subtle shift first. Most micromanagers don't respond well to sudden ultimatums.

Reinforce Positive Change: Reward the Retreat

When your micromanager backs off — even a little — acknowledge it. Positive reinforcement isn't just for dogs and toddlers.

"Thanks for giving me space to run with the report last week — I felt really empowered, and I think the results show that."

This not only reinforces the behavior you want, but also reframes their shift as a leadership strength — which they're more likely to embrace.

Set Internal Boundaries, Too

This chapter wouldn't be complete without a reminder that boundaries aren't just external. Micromanagement can sneak into your mind and turn into self-doubt. You start anticipating every critique before it happens, replaying conversations, or second-guessing your decisions.

Draw boundaries with yourself, too. Remind yourself: *"I'm not responsible for managing their anxiety — only my performance."* Journal your wins. Take breaks. Get perspective.

Because sometimes the biggest boundary is the one that keeps your self-worth separate from someone else's insecurity.

Final Thought: Boundaries Aren't Walls — They're Bridges

When done well, boundaries don't isolate. They connect. They make it clear where responsibilities begin and end. They create respect, reduce friction, and foster clarity.

With a micromanager, you're not erecting a fortress — you're building a bridge with signposts. You're saying, *"Here's how we can work together in a way that doesn't crush my soul or your sanity."*

In the next chapter, we'll talk about building trust — the golden currency that ultimately makes micromanagement obsolete (or at least, bearable).

Chapter 4: Building Trust – One Small Win at a Time

If micromanagement is fueled by anxiety and control, then trust is its antidote. Trust is what loosens the grip. It's the invisible force that tells your micromanager, *It's okay to let go.*

But here's the thing — trust isn't built in sweeping grand gestures. It's forged in small, consistent moments: a steady drip of reliability, honesty, and delivery. This chapter is about how to earn that trust — not through flattery or flinching compliance, but through authentic, strategic steps that slowly but surely change the dynamic.

Show Up Like Clockwork: Reliability Is the Foundation

Micromanagers are constantly looking for cracks. Miss a deadline, delay an update, or forget a detail, and you reinforce their worst fears. On the flip side, consistency becomes your secret weapon.

Deliver on your promises, hit your deadlines (or communicate early if you can't), and be on time for meetings. These might seem like basics, but in the eyes of a micromanager, they're gold.

Every time you show up prepared, you're silently saying, *I've got this.*

Celebrate the Small Wins – Loud Enough to Be Heard

You don't need to throw a party every time you finish a report. But you do want to gently surface your progress and wins.

This isn't about bragging — it's about strategic visibility. A quick message saying, *Task A is completed and already yielding some early results,* goes a long way. It gives them the dopamine hit of progress and reinforces their faith in you.

Think of this like breadcrumbing trust — one little nugget at a time.

Own Your Mistakes — But Control the Narrative

Trust doesn't mean being perfect. In fact, perfectionism can feel inauthentic. Real trust is built when you're honest about setbacks and handle them with maturity.

If something goes wrong, don't hide it or deflect. Acknowledge it briefly, explain the fix, and move on:

I missed the client's formatting request — already updated and re-sent the file. All good now.

Short. Calm. In control. This signals that you're accountable and solution-oriented — exactly the combo that earns trust.

Invite Input Before It's Demanded

Want to flip the script? Ask for feedback before they jump in.

Before I finalize this, would love your input on whether the tone aligns with what you had in mind.

This makes them feel involved (which they like), but on your terms (which you need). It shows confidence, not neediness — you're in control, just pulling them in strategically.
Bonus: when they feel consulted early, they often interfere less later.

Let Your Work Speak – But Turn Up the Volume

Many professionals make the mistake of assuming good work will speak for itself. And it does — sometimes. But with micromanagers, you often need to turn up the volume.

Don't assume they're noticing your smooth project execution in silence. Surface it in context:

Noticed our ticket resolution time dropped 15% this week — that's the new workflow we put in place kicking in.

Connect your work to measurable wins. This turns their attention from your process to your outcomes — which is the shift you want.

Document Like a Pro

Micromanagers fear chaos. So give them clarity.

Keep clean records. Summarize next steps after meetings. Send quick follow-up emails outlining agreed decisions. You're not over-documenting for the sake of it — you're creating a paper trail of competence, which calms their anxiety and builds confidence.

Be Transparent (But Not a Confessional)

Transparency builds trust, but that doesn't mean narrating your every thought or fear.

Be open about blockers, realistic about timelines, and honest about bandwidth — but skip the drama.

Instead of:

I'm overwhelmed and behind on everything.

Try:

I'm currently prioritizing X and Y to stay on track. Z might need a push to Thursday — will keep you posted.

You're still transparent, but you're steering the ship.

Pick Your Battles Wisely

Sometimes you'll need to push back. When you do, be strategic. Push back with data, with reason, and with calm:

I understand the urge to re-check the client emails, but they've been reviewed twice already, and resending could confuse them. Here's the last thread for reference — want to align on a consistent approach going forward?

That's not defiance. That's leadership. And leadership builds trust.

Don't Just Deliver – Overdeliver (Selectively)

Want to fast-track trust? Choose one or two moments to go above and beyond.

This isn't about working 80-hour weeks — it's about strategic excellence:

- Submit a report early with extra insight.
- Add unexpected value in a presentation.
- Anticipate a question before it's asked.

These moments create trust spikes — big jumps in confidence that often lead to greater freedom.

Mirror Their Priorities

If your micromanager worships KPIs, speak in KPIs. If they care about client satisfaction, weave that into your updates.

When you align your messaging with what they care about, it registers faster and deeper.

Trust equation:

This person gets what I care about = I can trust them more.

Final Thought: Trust Isn't a One-Time Event

You don't win trust like a trophy and walk away. It's more like a muscle — it builds with use, atrophies with neglect, and flexes differently depending on the situation.

But as trust grows, you'll feel the grip loosen. The check-ins fade. The freedom grows.

And your micromanager? They'll slowly stop micromanaging — not because you told them to, but because you showed them they didn't have to.

In the next chapter, we'll dive into the long game — how to build resilience and preserve your energy while you navigate (and outlast) micromanagement culture.

Chapter 5: Surviving the Long Game – Resilience in the Micromanagement Zone

Let's face it. Even the best strategies won't transform a chronic micromanager overnight. You could be the Zen master of pre-emptive communication, the boundary-setting ninja, and still find yourself bombarded with unnecessary check-ins on a Thursday at 7 p.m.

That's because micromanagement isn't just a behavior — it's often a culture. And navigating a culture takes more than tactics; it takes stamina.

In this chapter, we're going to focus on **you**. How do you stay sane, sharp, and motivated when you're working under someone who thinks supervision is a full-contact sport?

Here's your guide to surviving — and even thriving — in the long game.

Pace Yourself: You're in a Marathon, Not a Sprint

Dealing with micromanagement can be exhausting, and burnout is a real risk. Stop trying to "fix" everything in a week. Sustainable change takes time.

Know when to push and when to coast. Know which days to stand your ground and which days to just nod, smile, and save your energy for something more important.

Emotional energy is a finite resource. Spend it wisely.

Create Micro-Sanctuaries of Autonomy

Even in the most tightly managed environments, there are usually pockets of freedom. Find them. Protect them.

Maybe it's a recurring task that doesn't draw scrutiny, a low-stakes side project, or the first hour of your workday.

Use those moments to recharge your professional identity — the part of you that doesn't need oversight to function. They remind you who you are when nobody's watching.

Vent Strategically, Not Habitually

Venting feels good, but habitual venting can trap you in a cycle of helplessness.

Find a trusted colleague or mentor and set up a "constructive venting" session once a week. Focus on:

- What happened
- How it made you feel
- What you can try differently next time

End with action, not just exasperation.

Laugh When You Can

Micromanagement can be maddening — but also, sometimes, objectively hilarious. That fourth follow-up on a two-sentence email? Comedy gold.

Humor is a powerful buffer against stress. Turn the ridiculous moments into stories. Share them (safely). Laugh. It won't change the behavior, but it changes your relationship to the behavior.

Build Allies and Find Your People

You're probably not the only one being micromanaged.

Find others. Compare notes. Trade survival tips. Better yet, support each other. Offer to proofread that extra report. Give someone a heads-up on a meeting surprise.

Solidarity doesn't just make things easier — it reminds you you're not crazy.

Maintain a Parallel Identity

Your job is just one part of your life. If micromanagement is shrinking your role at work, don't let it shrink you.

Invest in areas that reinforce your confidence and independence:

- Volunteer
- Teach
- Build something
- Write

- Run
- Create

When your day job makes you feel small, your side gig reminds you how big your potential really is.

Stay Professionally Visible Outside Your Manager

Micromanagers often dominate the internal narrative about your performance. Make sure others see the full picture.

Share wins with stakeholders. Contribute to cross-functional projects. Volunteer insights during group meetings.

You're not bypassing your manager — you're diversifying your reputation portfolio.

Master the Art of Mental Boundaries

Sometimes the only boundary you can control is mental. Practice the fine art of emotionally detaching from overbearing supervision.

Don't internalize every comment. Don't carry their stress into your weekend. Don't mistake their panic for your failure.

Micromanagement is about them, not you. Keep that distinction sacred.

Document Everything (Yes, Still)

Good documentation isn't just for their peace of mind — it's for yours.

When things go sideways (and they will), having a clear record protects you, clarifies accountability, and helps you avoid unnecessary blame.

Documentation is the armor you wear while change is still catching up.

Know When to Walk Away

Some environments won't change. Some micromanagers will never loosen the reins. And no strategy in this book can justify sacrificing your mental health long-term.

If you've tried consistently and in good faith, and still feel stuck in a toxic loop — start exploring options. Quietly. Strategically. With dignity.

You're allowed to outgrow dysfunction.

Final Word: Survival Is Strength

You don't have to win every battle. You just have to outlast the chaos long enough to turn the page.

You're not weak for feeling drained — you're resilient for sticking it out while protecting your sense of self.

The micromanager may never change. But you will. And that change — that evolution into someone more patient, more self-aware, and more strategically communicative — is the win they'll never see coming.

In the next chapter, we'll explore how to flip the script — learning how to subtly influence your micromanager's behavior without them even realizing it. It's time to become a stealthy change agent.

Chapter 6: Stealth Mode – Influencing Without Triggering Alarms.

If you're still here, still breathing, and still managing to keep your inbox from imploding under the weight of "Just following up" messages, congratulations. You've done more than survive — you've endured. You've established boundaries, built trust, and even reclaimed small patches of peace. But what if I told you there's one more level?.

Welcome to stealth mode. The next evolution in your micromanager survival strategy isn't about defense. It's about subtle offense — shaping their behavior without ever confronting it head-on. Think of it as Jedi-level diplomacy: invisible nudges, strategic reframing, and psychological aikido.

Ready? Let's begin.

Redirect Their Energy Instead of Resisting It
Micromanagers often have a surplus of nervous energy. Rather than fighting that tide, redirect it into something more productive.

Example: Instead of just saying "I've got it handled," invite them to review something that needs their eye — a rough draft, a process improvement, or a template. Let them feel useful where their involvement doesn't derail you.

You're not indulging them. You're rerouting them.

Give Them Credit Strategically
Micromanagers often want recognition — for being involved, for keeping things on track, for being "hands-on." So give it to them… but in a way that builds your autonomy.

Try this: "Thanks to your input last week, I was able to get ahead on X — I've implemented your suggestion into my approach going forward."

This makes them feel acknowledged and creates space. You're subtly saying, *I heard you. I integrated. I've got it from here.*

Reframe Their Feedback Before It Lands
If you know their feedback style is intense, preframe it before they speak.

"I know you'll probably want me to focus on the formatting here — I've prepped a version with two options so we can pick the cleaner one."

This accomplishes two things: it reduces the sting of their feedback (because you've predicted it) and gives you control over the direction.

Make Their Wins Your Independence
Whenever a project goes well under your initiative, frame it as a mutual success.

"Glad we pulled that off so smoothly — I think the pre-check-in structure we've set up really helped me stay ahead."

Now you've turned your autonomy into a shared win. This isn't manipulation — it's narrative co-ownership. You're shaping the story.

Use the "Assumed Approval" Technique
Rather than asking "Can I…" — which invites more oversight — use language that assumes approval but leaves space for objections.

Instead of: "Can I send this to the client by noon?"
Try: "I'll send this over by noon unless there's anything you'd like to tweak."

This subtly shifts the power balance. It signals confidence while still respecting their authority.

Invite Strategic Input, Not Tactical Micromanagement
Frame your questions and requests in ways that elevate them to their role.

Ask: "What's the one thing you'd want senior leadership to notice about this project?"
Avoid: "Should I use green or blue in the chart?"

You're steering them toward vision-level input — which is where they should be — and away from pixel-pushing.

Offer Visibility Without Dependence
Micromanagers panic when they feel out of the loop. You can keep them informed without becoming dependent.

Share: “This week’s dashboard is live — feel free to check progress anytime.”

This provides reassurance without inviting critique. It’s a digital version of *You can look, but please don’t touch*.

Make Trust the Default Narrative
Speak as if trust already exists. Say: “I figured I’d take full ownership of this — I know you trust me to handle it.”

This makes distrust seem like a deviation from the norm, not the expectation. It subtly nudges them toward the version of themselves you want to work with.

Seed Future Autonomy
Use past wins to frame future independence.

“Since the last campaign ran so smoothly without extra reviews, I’ll run with the same level of autonomy this time too — should be even faster.”.

Here, you’re turning yesterday’s success into tomorrow’s freedom.

Be Their Mirror — Show the Behavior You Want
Finally, model the communication style you wish they used. Clear. Concise. Respectful. Collaborative.

When they micromanage, respond with: "Got it — I'll keep you looped in as needed. Here's the plan I'm following.".

They may not change overnight, but consistent modeling gives them an alternative rhythm to match.

Final Thought: Subtle Power is Still Power
Stealth mode isn't about manipulation — it's about influence. It's about choosing your battles and changing the temperature without setting off alarms.

By mastering this level of the game, you're not just coping — you're leading from within.

In the next chapter, we'll explore what to do when you become a manager yourself — how to break the cycle of micromanagement and become the leader you always wished you had.

Chapter 7: Breaking the Cycle – Becoming the Manager You Always Wanted

So, after all that micromanagement jiu-jitsu, here you are — either promoted, promoted soon, or simply determined to do things differently. You've seen what doesn't work.

You've lived it. You've been the mouse in the maze. And now? Now you get to redesign the maze.

Becoming a manager gives you a rare opportunity — the chance to stop the cycle of micromanagement before it starts. Not just for the sake of your sanity, but for your team's growth, morale, and performance.

So how do you build a management style rooted in trust, autonomy, and mutual respect?

How do you lead without hovering, guide without suffocating, and coach without commandeering?

Let's dive in.

Start With Self-Awareness: Micromanagement Begins in the Mirror

Every micromanager thinks they're just "being thorough." Or "making sure nothing falls through the cracks."

But before you do the same, ask yourself:

- Why do I feel the need to check in right now?
- Do I trust this person to do the work?
- Is this about their performance… or my anxiety?

Check your motives. Awareness is the first antidote.

Hire for Autonomy, Then Prove You Mean It

If you hire someone for their initiative, don't squash it the moment they show it.

Let them run with ideas. Let them experiment. Let them fail and recover. Then reward the process of ownership, not just the outcome.

The fastest way to lose a high-performer? Hover over their shoulder.

Make Delegation a Dialogue

Delegation doesn't mean dumping. It means aligning.

Instead of saying, "Just do this," try: "Here's the outcome we need. What's your approach?"

Then shut up. Let them explain. If their plan is sound — or even just not disastrous — let them run with it.

Define Outcomes, Not Instructions

Your job isn't to script every step. It's to clarify the destination.

Instead of: "Use this template. Write it this way." Say: "We need to communicate A, B, and C by Friday. However you get there — just make sure it's clear, concise, and on-brand."

Give freedom within clear fences.

Build a Culture of Check-ins, Not Check-ups

Regular updates are good. Surveillance is not.

Create a predictable rhythm of check-ins that feel like support, not interrogation.

Ask:

- "What's working?"
- "What's stuck?"
- "Where can I help?"

And when things are going smoothly? Just say: "Keep going — you've got this."

Share the 'Why' Behind the 'What'

People work better when they know the context.

Explain the bigger picture: “This task connects to the product launch, which affects Q4 goals. Your part matters because it influences user adoption.”

That context fuels motivation — and trust.

Give Feedback That Feeds Confidence

When things go well, say so. Publicly, if possible. Highlight their judgment, their initiative, their ownership.

When giving constructive feedback, focus on course correction, not blame. And always tie it back to growth: “This didn’t land as expected — but I know you’ll adapt. Let’s think through the next version together.”

Encourage Risk, Celebrate Recovery

You can’t say, “Take risks!” and then punish every mistake.

Instead, say: “Try something bold — I’ve got your back.”

And when it fails? “Great learning. What’s next?”

This builds psychological safety — the antidote to micromanagement.

Let Go of the Illusion of Control

Here’s a truth bomb: control is a myth. At best, it’s a comforting delusion.

Great managers don't aim for control. They aim for clarity. Alignment. Trust.

Control exhausts everyone. Clarity empowers them.

Remember What It Felt Like

Never forget the cramped, stifling feeling of being micromanaged.

Channel that memory into empathy. Into patience. Into a quiet vow:
"I will never make my team feel that small."

Final Word: You Hold the Pen Now

You've turned every page, survived every chapter.

You've navigated, endured, and adapted. And now, you're the one writing the story — not just for yourself, but for those who look to you for leadership.

Make it a story of trust. Of courage. Of letting go — and watching your team rise.

In the next chapter, we'll tackle what to do when micromanagement comes from peers, not superiors. Yes, lateral micromanagement is real, and it's a whole different kind of challenge.

Chapter 8: When Peers Hover – Dealing with Lateral Micromanagement

Just when you thought you had the micromanagement menace cornered, it sneaks in from the side.

You've handled the boss who wants hourly updates. You've set boundaries, built trust, maybe even earned some autonomy.

But now — surprise — it's your peer, your colleague, your supposed equal who's stepping on your toes. They're reviewing your slides like they're your manager. They're "just checking in" on a task you clearly own. They're forwarding emails you're already on, with "friendly reminders."

Welcome to the strange world of lateral micromanagement — the unsolicited oversight from someone at your level, but acting like they're your supervisor.

It's annoying. It's confusing. And left unchecked, it can poison collaboration. But fear not — you can navigate this too. Let's dive in.

1. Recognize the Breed: Helpful or Hovering? Not all unsolicited involvement is malicious. Sometimes, it's just overzealous "helpfulness." But the line between supportive and suffocating is thinner than you'd think.

Ask yourself: Is this person adding clarity or clutter? Are they genuinely collaborating, or trying to control? Is their "help" improving outcomes or just doubling the work?

If their input feels more like interference than assistance, you're likely dealing with lateral micromanagement.

2. Understand Their Motivation.
Just like with traditional micromanagers, peer-hovering often stems from their own insecurities or pressures.

Are they under pressure to "lead" without formal authority?
Do they fear being sidelined or made irrelevant? Are they trying to impress someone up the chain?

Understanding their "why" doesn't excuse the behavior — but it helps you respond strategically instead of emotionally.

3. Hold Your Ground, Gently.
The trickiest part? You can't pull the "I report to someone else" card — because they're not your boss. And you don't want to create open conflict.

Instead, use subtle boundary-setting language:
"Thanks, I've got this one covered."
"Appreciate the input — I'll loop you in once the first draft's ready."
"I'm sticking to the approach we aligned on. Happy to compare notes later if needed."

Short, firm, polite. No need to over-explain. Just nudge them back to their lane.

4. Create Clarity Through Ownership.
Micromanagement thrives in ambiguity. If you're unclear about who owns what, people will start stepping into your territory — or expect you to report on theirs.

Proactively clarify roles: "I'll take lead on this section; you handle the implementation piece."
"Let's divide and conquer — I'll own the delivery, you focus on prep."

Then document it, even in a casual follow-up message or shared workspace. Clear accountability reduces territorial squabbles.

5. Preempt Their Urge with Updates.
If they hover because they're worried things will fall through the cracks, beat them to the punch.

Send short, confident updates: "Just wrapped up the outline — will share by 3pm."
"Talked to the vendor, all set for Friday."

This builds trust and reduces their need to check in constantly. It also shifts the narrative — you're not avoiding responsibility; you're ahead of it.

6. Loop Them In — But On Your Terms.
Sometimes, peer micromanagers just want to feel

included. Instead of shutting them out entirely, give them controlled windows of participation.

“Hey, I’ll share the draft once the key points are locked.”
“Can you review this section specifically? Your input would help there.”

This gives them a role — but not the whole stage.

7. Don’t Take the Bait.
Passive-aggressive comments, constant corrections, veiled “suggestions”? Don’t engage emotionally.

Resist the urge to clap back. Respond with calm professionalism. If needed, escalate through the appropriate channels — but only with evidence and after you've tried everything else.

Preserve your energy. Don’t wrestle with shadows.

8. Protect Your Reputation.
One danger of peer micromanagement is that it can quietly undermine your perceived competence. If someone’s always “fixing” your work or double-checking everything, others might assume you’re dropping the ball — even when you’re not.

That’s why it’s important to:
Document your contributions clearly.
Speak confidently in meetings.
Let your work speak loudly — and visibly — for itself.

Visibility is your shield. Use it.

9. Build Strategic Alliances.
You don't have to fight this alone. Talk to others — respectfully — about working norms. You might discover you're not the only one experiencing the peer-hover.

If that's the case, a team-wide discussion on ownership, autonomy, and collaboration norms might be in order. Sometimes, the best antidote to micromanagement is team clarity.

10. Know When It's Time for a Bigger Conversation.
If the peer's behavior is affecting your work, your morale, or the team's output — and subtle nudges haven't worked — it might be time to escalate.

Frame it not as a complaint but as a concern: "I value collaboration, but I've noticed some recurring overlap in responsibilities with [Name], and it's starting to create inefficiencies. Can we clarify roles moving forward?"

Stay focused on outcomes and solutions. Keep your tone constructive, not personal.

Lateral Doesn't Mean Lesser
Peer micromanagement may not come with a title, but its impact can be just as disruptive. The key is handling it with grace, strategy, and a firm sense of your own value.

You don't need to defend every move. But you do need to protect your space.

Remember: confidence, clarity, and calm go a long way.

In the next chapter, we'll explore how to navigate micromanagement in remote or hybrid environments — where the digital leash can feel even tighter.

Chapter 9: Digital Chains – Micromanagement in the Remote Era

Working from home used to sound like a dream, didn't it? Pajamas all day. No commute. Coffee from your favorite mug. Freedom.

And then… Slack messages at 9:02 a.m. Calendar invites with no agenda. "Just checking in" Zoom calls that feel like parole hearings. Google Docs with more comments than content.

Suddenly, that freedom feels more like a digital leash.

Welcome to micromanagement in the remote era — where distance doesn't dilute control, it sometimes amplifies it.

Let's unpack how to survive and thrive when micromanagement comes through Wi-Fi.

Understand the Remote Control Complex

In an office, a micromanager could physically walk by your desk. They could pop into meetings, hover, ask for updates in passing.

Remote work takes that power away.
So what happens?
They double down digitally.

More pings. More meetings. More "status check" emails. It's not that they've suddenly become worse — they've just lost their crutches and are trying to regain control in the only way they know how.

Understanding this isn't about excusing the behavior — it's about strategizing your response.

Set Communication Cadence Early

The number one way to prevent virtual micromanagement?
Establish clear communication norms from the beginning.

- When will you check in?
- What format will updates take?
- What channels should be used for what?

Example:

"Let's align on one weekly check-in call and a Monday/Thursday progress update via email. Urgent stuff can go on Slack."

This makes communication feel planned, not chaotic. Predictability lowers anxiety — and micromanagers are fueled by anxiety.

Use Visibility Tools to Your Advantage

Remote work lacks visibility, and that's where micromanagement thrives.

Use shared tools — not to let them breathe down your neck, but to proactively show progress:

- A well-maintained Trello board
- A clean Asana task list
- A shared progress doc updated weekly

The goal is transparency without interruption. Micromanagers want control — you give them visibility. It's not the same, but it scratches their itch just enough to back off.

The Magic of the End-of-Day Ping

One powerful trick: the EOD ping.

A short message at the end of each day — or at regular intervals — such as:

"Wrapped up the proposal draft today. Tomorrow morning I'll review it and send it your way by noon."

It's not lengthy. It's not reporting for duty. It's just a friendly wave that says: *I've got this.*

Do it consistently, and watch how the random "how's it going?" messages magically disappear.

Push Asynchronous Culture (Without Sounding Lazy)

If your micromanager wants real-time responses for everything, they're turning remote work into a digital office — with more interruptions and fewer snacks.

Help shift toward async culture by:

- Using scheduled messages and email summaries
- Proposing Slack-free focus hours
- Logging updates where they can be read, not just heard

Example:

"Sharing the update here so it's documented — feel free to reply when convenient!"

It encourages thoughtful responses instead of panic-pings.

Clarify Expectations and Deliverables

Ambiguity is the breeding ground for micromanagement — especially remotely.

Get crystal clear on:

- What the exact deliverable is
- The deadline
- Review points

Once defined, confirm in writing:

"Just to align — I'll deliver the final version by EOD Friday. No check-ins needed unless anything shifts on your end."

That's polite, professional, and quietly firm.

Fight Fire with Documentation

If you feel like you're being second-guessed or nitpicked, document your work trail.

No need to create a novella — just build a paper trail of decisions, updates, and confirmations. It's not about covering your back. It's about quietly proving you're in control.

It also helps when that inevitable, "Didn't we agree on X?" moment arises. You'll be ready — receipts in hand.

Use Video Calls Strategically, Not Frequently

A daily Zoom isn't always necessary — it's often just a security blanket for your micromanager.

Push for fewer, more meaningful meetings:

- Propose agenda-driven calls
- Bundle updates into one conversation
- Use screen shares to walk them through progress visually

Better one strong 30-minute call than five "just checking" five-minute ones.

Respect Time Zones, Calendars, and Mental Space

Remote doesn't mean 24/7. Micromanagers may unconsciously blur boundaries because they can't see when you're off the clock.

Set those expectations clearly:

- Use calendar blocks like "Deep Work – Do Not Disturb"
- Mute after-hours pings (and don't respond unless urgent)
- Include working hours in your email signature or Slack status

Boundaries don't set themselves — you have to build them, and honor them.

Practice Screen Presence Without Being Always Online

You don't need to hover on Zoom or green-dot Slack all day.

Be responsive, not reactive.
Let your work do the talking.
Let your systems show your flow.

Remember: presence isn't about blinking online — it's about being visible in meaningful, consistent ways.

Remote ≠ Helpless

You're not at the mercy of Wi-Fi warriors and Slack snipers.

Remote micromanagement feels different, but it can still be managed. With the right structure, proactive communication, and digital boundaries, you can regain control of your day — and your sanity.

Your screen is not your cage. It can be your stage.

Chapter 10: When to Fold 'Em – Recognizing When It's Time to Leave

Let’s face it — not every workplace can be saved. And not every micromanager can be tamed.

Sometimes, despite your best communication tactics, trust-building efforts, and Jedi level diplomacy, the environment remains toxic. The micromanagement doesn’t wane — it worsens.

You find yourself dreading Mondays, second-guessing every move, and feeling like a ghost in your own career.

This chapter is your reality check — and your permission slip. It’s about recognizing when the battle is no longer worth it and when it's time to walk away with your head high.

The Signs You’re Not Just Being Tested – You’re Being Crushed

It’s normal to face challenges at work. But prolonged micromanagement that turns into emotional wear-and-tear is a red flag. Watch for these signs:

- Your stress levels remain high outside of work.
- You’ve stopped growing or learning anything new.
- You’re constantly questioning your competence.

- You feel physically or mentally exhausted — even on weekends.
- You dread interacting with your manager.
- You're dreaming of any other job — even one that pays less — just to escape.

These are not badges of resilience. These are burnout signals.

You've Tried Everything, and Nothing's Changing

If you've gone through the playbook — set boundaries, communicated proactively, documented like a court reporter — and nothing has improved, then it's time to step back and ask:

Is this just who they are? Is this how the culture is? Am I spending energy trying to fix something that doesn't want to be fixed?

Micromanagement isn't always a personal flaw. Sometimes it's cultural — embedded in leadership, systems, and performance norms. If that's the case, even the best employee can't change it alone.

The Cost is Greater Than the Paycheck

Money is important — no doubt. But it's not worth your health, your self-esteem, or your sense of purpose.

Calculate the true cost:

- How much are you spending emotionally to earn your paycheck?
- How many nights have you lost sleep?
- How many relationships or hobbies have suffered?

If you're paying with your peace, that's not a paycheck — it's a ransom.

You're Losing Yourself

One of the sneakiest effects of chronic micromanagement is identity erosion. You start to forget what you're good at. You mute your opinions. You feel smaller. Duller. Like your light is dimming a little each day.

When a job starts shaping who you are — in all the wrong ways — it's not just about career anymore. It's about self-preservation.

The Opportunity Cost is Too High

Every moment you spend under a suffocating micromanager is a moment not spent growing, leading, learning, and evolving somewhere else.

Imagine if that energy were redirected. What could you build? Who could you become?

Opportunity cost isn't just a finance term — it's a life metric.

You Deserve Better (Really)

It's easy to forget this when you're knee-deep in frustration, but it's true: You deserve to be trusted. You deserve space to shine.

You deserve leadership that lifts you, not limits you.

Sometimes the bravest move isn't enduring. It's exiting.

Making the Leap – Planning Your Exit Strategically

Quitting doesn't have to be dramatic. It can be thoughtful, graceful, and even empowering.

Steps to take:

- Update your resume — even if you're just exploring.
- Reach out to your network quietly.
- Set a timeline for when you'll reassess your situation.
- Save a cushion if possible.
- Reflect on what you truly want next — not just what you want to escape from.

You're not running away. You're walking toward better.

Know This: You're Not the Problem

Micromanagers often leave a trail of doubt.

You might wonder if you're too sensitive, too slow, too resistant.

But hear this clearly: Micromanagement is about control — not your capability. If you've given your best and still feel stuck, the problem isn't you. The system is broken. And sometimes, the only fix is to remove yourself from the system.

Your Exit Isn't a Failure – It's a Graduation

Leaving a micromanaged environment isn't quitting. It's choosing growth over stagnation. Sanity over scrutiny. Light over shadow.

Some chapters aren't meant to be rewritten. They're meant to end — so you can start a better one.

In the final chapter, we'll reflect on the journey — not just how to survive micromanagement, but how to thrive in its aftermath. Because life beyond the microscope? It's waiting. And it's beautiful.

Chapter 11: Life After the Microscope – Thriving Beyond Micromanagement

If you've made it this far, congratulations — not only have you survived the world of micromanagement, you've also proven you're serious about transforming the way you work and lead.

And now? It's time to go beyond survival.

This final chapter isn't about dodging check-ins or crafting clever updates. It's about your next chapter — one where you thrive in autonomy-rich environments, inspire trust, and become the kind of leader (or teammate) others wish they had. One where your scars turn into wisdom, and your resilience becomes a blueprint for others.

Rebuilding Your Confidence

Micromanagement can chip away at your self-worth. It's time to reverse that.

- Take stock of your strengths — the ones you may have muted.
- Reflect on the situations you handled with grace and poise.
- Remind yourself: you're capable, you're smart, and you made it through the micro gauntlet.

Relearning How to Fly Solo

Ironically, micromanagement can make you overly reliant on someone else's input. Now’s your time to relearn freedom.

- Embrace decision-making.
- Make mistakes without shame.
- Experiment, innovate, and lead with your own flair.

Becoming a Beacon for Others

You’ve seen the dark side of bad management. Use it as fuel.

- Model trust and autonomy for others.
- Be the kind of leader who checks in without hovering.
- Champion a culture where people grow, not shrink.

Spotting the Warning Signs in Future Jobs

With experience comes wisdom. You now know what a micromanager looks like. Use it to your advantage.

- Ask smart questions in interviews.
- Pay attention to team dynamics.
- Choose cultures that prioritize empowerment.

Celebrating the Journey

Don't rush into the next hustle. Pause. Celebrate.

- Acknowledge your growth.
- Appreciate your grit.
- Share your story — because you never know who needs to hear it.

The End Is Just the Beginning

You've learned the language of the micromanager, survived the close calls, and built a toolkit of strategies.

But more than that — you've developed the one thing that matters most: awareness.

Awareness of your boundaries. Awareness of your worth. Awareness of how to protect your peace and power.

That awareness? It will serve you long after this book ends.

So go out there. Thrive loudly. Lead wisely. And if you ever feel someone tying your metaphorical shoelaces again. smile, untie them, and keep running.

Your autonomy isn't just a goal. It's your new normal.

Thank you for reading this book. I hope you enjoyed the journey, learned a few survival tricks, and most importantly — rediscovered your power.